Awesome Abs

The Body Coach Series

Awesome Abs

Build your leanest midsection ever with

Australia's Body Coach®

Paul Collins

Meyer & Meyer Sports

British Library Cataloguing in Publication Data
A catalogue record for this book is available from the British Library

Paul Collins
Awesome Abs
Maidenhead: Meyer & Meyer Sport (UK) Ltd., 2008
ISBN 978-1-84126-232-1

© 2008 by Paul Collins (text & photos) and Meyer & Meyer Sport (UK) Ltd. (Layout)
Aachen, Adelaide, Auckland, Budapest, Graz, Indianapolis, Johannesburg, Maidenhead,
New York, Olten (CH), Singapore, Toronto
Member of the World
Sport Publishers' Association (WSPA)
www.w-s-p-a.org

Printed and bound by: B.O.S.S Druck und Medien GmbH, Germany
ISBN 978-1-84126-232-1
E-Mail: verlag@m-m-sports.com
www.m-m-sports.com

Introduction

Welcome!

I'm The Body Coach, Paul Collins, your exclusive personal coach here to guide and motivate towards building your leanest midsection ever. The abdominal muscles, commonly referred to as abs, midsection, core region, six-pack or center-of-power, are one of the most prized assets to any physique. A rock-hard midsection is the goal for anyone who exercises regularly as it provides the finishing touch to an impressive physique.

Awesome Abs features practical, easy to follow exercises for achieving a leaner midsection, stronger lower back, better posture and trimmer waistline. The abdominal muscles, while normally sought after for aesthetic purposes, serve a critical function in daily movement, sport, physical activity and posture. More importantly a strong midsection helps support and protect your lower back region from injury.

For sport, a well conditioned mid-section allows you to change direction faster, generate force quicker, and absorb blows better. So, if you're an athlete looking for that extra edge, a fitness enthusiast looking to improve your physique or posture or a mom wanting to restrengthen her midsection after childbirth, Awesome Abs is for you.

Awesome Abs provides practical hands-on training to help:

- Tone and shape the midriff
- Trim the waistline in line with a healthy diet
- Strengthen the abdominal muscles
- Improve posture and reduce lower back injuries
- Reshape a woman's midsection after childbirth

Packed with over 70 exercises and tests using one's own body weight as well as fitness balls, medicine balls and abdominal machines, The Body Coach® Awesome Abs is ideal for athletes, sports persons and fitness enthusiasts alike of all age groups. It provides the building blocks from static strength through to core-power with its revolutionary **5 Phase Abdominal Training System**. I have also included 13 abdominal exercise training routines for specific target areas, postnatal and sports-specific training that can easily be carried out at home, in the gym or whilst travelling. Most importantly, you now have a program of exercises within easy reach for building your leanest midsection ever.

I look forward to working with you!
Paul Collins
The Body Coach®

A special thank you goes to:
Mark Donaldson (Photography), Nigel Rowden, Carlos Carlan, Marie Vodna; Athletes – Pat Daley, Alicia King, Linda Collins and Paul Bulatao; AASF Sydney Staff Paul, Catherine and Senko.

Contents

About the Author

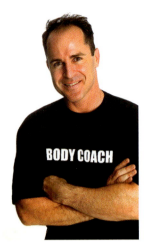

Paul Collins is an award-winning personal trainer in Australia, a prolific author on fitness and weight loss topics and general manager of the Australian Academy of Sport and Fitness, an International College in Sydney, Australia, specifically for overseas students wishing to study and obtain fitness and personal training qualifications. His trademark coaching has been pioneered from a remarkable recovery from a chronic lower back injury, without drugs or surgery – inspiring thousands of people through appearances on TV, radio and print media.

Coaching since age 14, Paul has personally trained world-class athletes and teams in a variety of sports, e.g., athletics, rugby, soccer, squash, tennis and many others including members of the Australian Olympic and Paralympic Swimming Teams. He is also a key presenter for the Australian Track and Field Coaching Association, Australian Swimming Coaches and Teachers Association, NSW Squash Academy and the Australian Fitness Industry.

Paul is an outstanding athlete in his own right, having played grade level in the national rugby league competition. He is also a former Australian Budokan Karate Champion, A-grade squash player and NSW Masters Athletics Track & Field State Champion. As a leader in the field of personal fitness and weight loss, Paul has successfully combined a sports fitness background with Bachelor of Physical Education degree and international certification as a strength and conditioning coach and personal trainer. As designer of *The Body Coach* book series, exercise products and educational programs, Paul travels internationally to present a highly entertaining series of corporate health & well-being seminars and exclusive five-star personal training for VIPs.

To learn more visit: www.thebodycoach.com

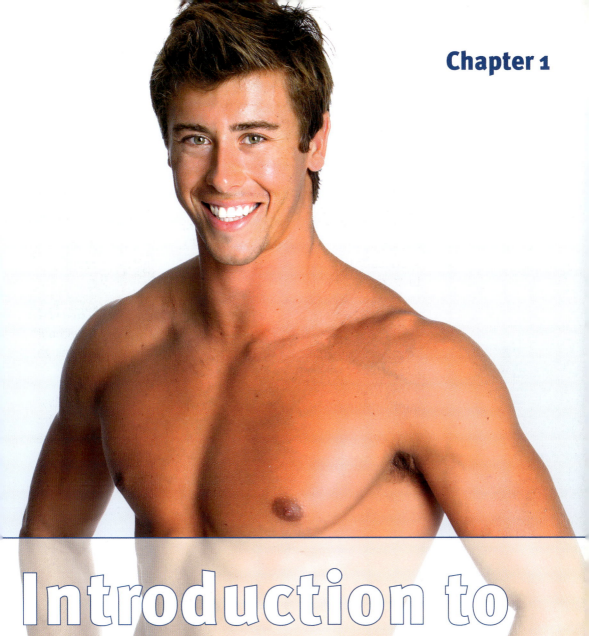

Chapter 1

Introduction to the Abdominal Region

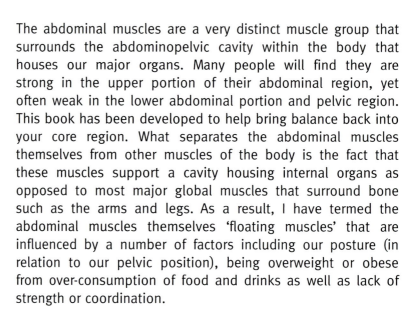

The abdominal muscles are a very distinct muscle group that surrounds the abdominopelvic cavity within the body that houses our major organs. Many people will find they are strong in the upper portion of their abdominal region, yet often weak in the lower abdominal portion and pelvic region. This book has been developed to help bring balance back into your core region. What separates the abdominal muscles themselves from other muscles of the body is the fact that these muscles support a cavity housing internal organs as opposed to most major global muscles that surround bone such as the arms and legs. As a result, I have termed the abdominal muscles themselves 'floating muscles' that are influenced by a number of factors including our posture (in relation to our pelvic position), being overweight or obese from over-consumption of food and drinks as well as lack of strength or coordination.

Obtaining good abdominal control and core-strength requires more than meets the eye. A healthy eating plan takes precedence in order to trim the waistline and improve the body's center of gravity. Combined with regular exercise, controlling calorie intake also helps reduce body fat levels that are primarily found around waistline. Muscles of the hip and gluteal (butt) region also need to be free of tension to ensure good pelvic mobility through regular stretching, massage and physical therapy. Increasing body awareness and understanding of your neutral spine position allows effective abdominal strength gains to occur when exercised. Exercises themselves are progressed through a series of core-isometric bracing and breathing exercises to build static postural endurance together with coordination exercises involving the arms and legs to further challenge the core. This is then followed by exercises for developing specific strength and power through the abdominal region. This progression is established via the 5 Phase Abdominal training program provided in the following chapters.

Getting to Know Your Abdominal Muscles

To effectively exercise the abdominal muscles it is important to understand each muscle within the abdominal framework and their primary functions.

MUSCLE	ORIGIN	INSERTION	PRIMARY FUNCTIONS
Rectus abdominis (six-pack)	Pubic crest	Cartilage of fifth through seventh ribs and xiphoid process	Flexion and lateral flexion of trunk
External oblique	Anteriolateral borders of lower eight ribs	Anterior half of ilium, pubic crest, and anterior fascia	Lateral flexion of the trunk
Internal oblique	Iliac crest	Cartilage of last three to four ribs	Lateral flexion of the trunk
Transverse abdominus (deepest muscle layer)	Iliac crest, lumbar fascia, and cartilages of last six ribs	Xiphoid process of sternum, anterior fascia, and pubis	Compresses abdomen
Erector spinae (back muscle)	Posterior iliac crest and sacrum	Angles of ribs, transverse processes of all ribs	Extension of trunk

Back

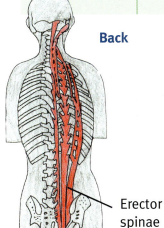

Erector spinae

Front

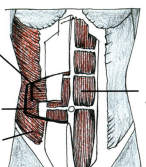

Transversus abdominis

Rectus abdominis

Internal oblique

External oblique

The Hip Muscles

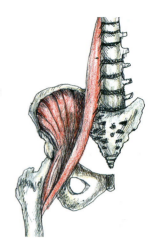

In addition to the specific abdominal muscles, one must also be aware of the influence that the iliopsoas and hip muscles have on the lower back, spine and pelvic positioning. The hip flexors are on the front of the hip and work to bend the hip and lift the leg, for example, a ballet dancer raising their leg or an athlete running fast with high knees. Because parts of these muscles attach to the back and spine, tightness in these muscles can lead to lower back pain, sacroiliac, groin or hip tension. Hence, it is vitally important to keep the hip and gluteal (butt) region free of muscular tension to allow for effective abdominal strength gains. Regular stretching, massage and physical therapy plays a vital role in maintaining a pliable hip framework and good posture required for maximal strength gains.

Exercising the Abdominal Muscles

The abdominal region is composed of internal and external muscles. The external muscles are known as the rectus abdominis and the external obliques. One of the best ways to train the rectus abdominis is by flexing your spine forward, commonly referred too as crunching or curling. Crunching forward, one-third of the way up, targets the entire rectus abdominis. Once the movement goes past this active zone, your hip flexors also come into play. Your obliques are targeted to a greater degree when any twisting action takes place, such as where you bring your elbow to the opposite knee. One of the best ways to train the transversus abdominis muscle is to simply pull your navel into your spine and exhale through pursed lips whilst keeping the stomach pulled in.

Preactivity Stretching

Good pelvic alignment is essential for optimal abdominal strength gains. Preactivity stretching focuses on bringing attention to correct pelvic alignment and body positioning. A warm-up may include a 5-minute brisk walk and abdominal bracing drills followed by stretching of muscles that surround or attach to the spine and pelvic regions.

This ensures the body is warm and free of tension helping maximize abdominal strength gains. The following 7 stretches can be used. Hold each stretch or position for up to 15 seconds without tension or pain. See The Body Coach Stretching Basics book for more details:

1. Thigh
Flex one knee and raise your heel to your buttocks. Slightly flex your supporting leg and grasp your raised foot. Gently pull heel towards buttock. Repeat with opposite leg.

2. Hamstrings
Extend one leg forward and rest on heel and bend the rear knee. Place both hands on forward thigh and gently lean forward ensuring toes are raised off the ground.

3. Side Bend
Stand with feet shoulder-width apart and hands on hips. Extend one arm overhead and bend to opposite side and hold. Repeat on opposite side.

4. Hip Flexors

Extend one leg back, lower body and rest on rear knee and toes. With front leg bent, place hands across thigh and keep tall. Bend forward knee and lower hip towards ground. Repeat on opposite side.

5. Hip, Lower Back and Deep Gluteal

Lie on your back with your right leg crossed over your left knee. Reach right arm through legs and left arm outside and grab the front of the knee and pull your legs towards your chest and hold. Repeat with opposite leg raised.

6. Hip, Gluteal and Mid Back

Sit on floor with hands behind back. Cross your right foot over your left leg. Grab your bent leg with left arm and gently twist body to the right side and hold. Repeat on opposite side.

7. Lower Back Raise on Forearms

Lie on your stomach with arms bent by your side and head resting on your fists. Gently brace abdominal muscles and slowly rise onto forearms keeping spine long, then lower.

Neutral Spine Position

All exercises have a number of key elements to consider when setting up and performing a movement. Applying correct technique from the onset will help strengthen muscles that support the spine, improve posture, breathing and functional movement patterns. That's why training the abdominal muscles is not just about looking good, but improving one's posture and maintaining a healthy spine for better mobility.

The spine is one of the most important parts of your body. It gives your body structure and support. It allows you to move about freely and to bend with flexibility. The spine is also designed to protect your spinal cord, a column of nerves that connects your brain with the rest of your body, allowing you to control your movements. Without a spinal cord, you could not move any part of your body, and your organs could not function. This is why keeping your spine healthy is very important.

Your spine is made up of 24 bones (vertebrae) that are positioned on top of one another forming a series of curves that form the spinal column. Between each vertebra is a soft, gel-like cushion called a disc that helps absorb pressure and keeps the bones from rubbing against each other. Each vertebra is held to the others by groups of ligaments. Ligaments connect bones to bones; tendons connect muscles to bones. There are also tendons that fasten muscles to the vertebrae. The spinal column also has facet joints that link the vertebrae together and give them the flexibility to move against each other.

Three main functions of the spine include:

1. Protecting the spinal cord
2. Supporting the body in an upright position
3. Allowing movement and locomotion

To help improve the health of our spine, it is important to develop better awareness of our body position by practicing the neutral spine position. The term neutral spine refers to the natural curvature (alignment) of the spine.

The main curves are:

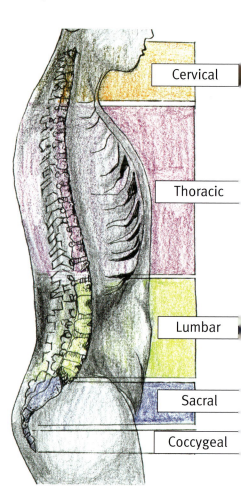

- **Cervical spine:**
  the rear of the neck curves slightly inwards

- **Thoracic spine:**
  the upper to mid area of the back curves slightly outwards

- **Lumbar spine:**
  the lower back curves slightly inwards

- **Sacral spine:**
  the bottom of your spine curves slightly outwards and links to the coccyx

Cervical

Thoracic

Lumbar

Sacral

Coccygeal

As you begin to move your spine and pelvis through a range of motion you will find a midpoint, one that activates the muscles that support the spine and makes you feel elongated and comfortable with the blood flowing more comfortably to the brain. When lying on your back with your knees bent, it can be helpful to gently flatten the back to the ground, then arch the back upwards and then fall comfortably between the two to find neutral position – as shown below:

Position 1
Gently tilt your pelvis backwards, flattening your lower back into the floor.

Position 2
Gently tilt your pelvis in the opposite direction, creating an arch under your lower back.

Position 3
Find a position between these two extremes in which your back feels natural and comfortable: this is the 'neutral spine' position.

Abdominal Bracing

To develop good body awareness and control of the abdominal region we introduce the 'Abdominal Bracing' technique. Abdominal bracing refers to drawing in the stomach region towards the spine and holding whilst exercising. The participant continues to breathe deeply whilst exercising and without losing the abdominal brace position which is held at around 50% of maximum voluntary contraction. In many cases, it is a matter of continually readjusting this brace position to ensure that the quality of the exercise is maintained. Initially, breathing may feel short and the stomach hard to hold in, but with practice you will improve your ability to contract your stomach muscles and breathe more efficiently, without tensing other muscles of the body.

Breathing Patterns

Drawing in air deeply through the nose and breathing out in a controlled manner with constant flow through the mouth through pursed lips, like blowing out candles, provides a good breathing platform of oxygen being taken into the bloodstream more efficiently whilst the muscles' waste product carbon dioxide is expelled.

Breathing should be used to control the rate of repetition of movement of the exercises in most cases. For instance, in the abdominal slide exercise, breathe out as you raise the body and exert a force and breathe in as you lower the body in recovery.

ABDOMINAL BRACING POSITIONS

2 Lying on Your Back

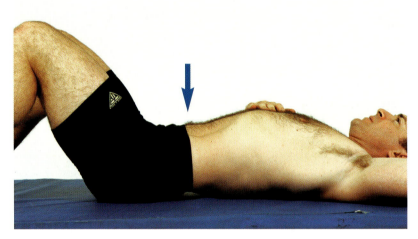

Draw abdominal muscles inwards whilst maintaining a neutral spine position

INSTRUCTION

- Lie on your back with knees bent maintaining neutral spine position.

- Brace abdominal muscles and hold.

- Your aim is to focus on the inwards contraction of the stomach without releasing for a set time frame or controlled number of breaths.

THE BODY COACH

ABDOMINAL BRACING POSITIONS

Sitting

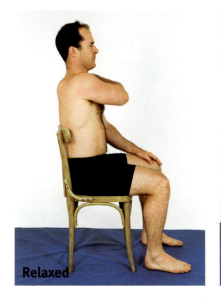

Relaxed

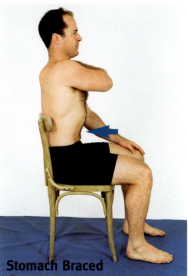

Stomach Braced

INSTRUCTION

- In a seated position, take a deep breath inwards, through your nose then as you breathe out through your mouth, draw your navel (belly button) inwards towards your spine and hold without changing your neutral spine position.
- Continue breathing in your nose and out your mouth deeply, whilst holding your stomach in, for 5 breaths, before releasing stomach.

Note: *Imagine placing a belt around your waist in line with your navel. Pulling your tummy in requires you to tighten the belt as the waist becomes thinner. The aim of abdominal bracing is to maintain a thin waistline whilst breathing deeply and exercising. Over time as strength, coordination and body awareness improves, this action will become automatic.*

ABDOMINAL BRACING POSITIONS

4 Four-Point Kneeling

Relaxed

Stomach Braced

INSTRUCTION

- In the four-point kneeling position (on your hands and knees), take a deep breath inwards through your nose, then as you breathe out through your mouth, draw your navel (belly button) inwards towards your spine and hold without changing your neutral spine position.
- Using big, deep breaths continue breathing in your nose and out your mouth whilst holding this braced position (stomach in), for 5 breaths. Relax and repeat.

Note: *Practice this braced position whilst sitting, kneeling, lying, standing, lifting, carrying, moving and exercising.*

THE BODY COACH

Abdominal Bracing Progression

As we introduce movement of the arms and legs into the equation when performing abdominal exercises we challenge the abdominal brace position. The abdominal brace is important because it helps reduce the load placed on the lower back region in both exercise and daily movement. Initially breathing may be short, but over time will become deeper as the diaphragm muscles strengthen and coordination improves. Deep breathing is important in every exercise helping improve body awareness, lung capacity and oxygen exchange. The goal of abdominal bracing is to bring attention to the correct body position with the focus on bracing and breathing in a relaxed manner.

Practice various abdominal bracing intensities to build good body awareness. Vary your abdominal bracing contraction between 30-50% of maximum holding contraction. Increase the time you hold this position by the number of deep breaths you perform or number of sets. Remember, as you breathe out, aim to maintain the tension of the stomach muscles without changing the position of the lower back or contracting the buttock muscles. The challenge to the abdominal brace comes from introducing exercises that involve movement of the arms or legs or both together. Learning to hold the abdominal brace whilst performing arm or leg movement in a variety of positions helps improve motor coordination. In various exercises the lower back is challenged and requires a strong abdominal brace to be held until the repetitions are completed. Ultimately, abdominal bracing helps maintain good posture when exercising and the ability to build endurance, which is required before speed or power movements of the arms or legs are introduced.

The weighted arm extension is one exercise used involving the arms and abdominal region to improve coordination. The weight held in the hands is light (i.e. medicine ball) and the movements are performed slowly. This is so the focus is placed on maintaining a strong abdominal brace and neutral spine position at all times whilst building essential body awareness for better muscle synergy, as follows:

5 Weighted Arm Extension

Target Area –
Abdominal
brace
through arm
coordination

Start

Midpoint

INSTRUCTION

- Lie on your back with knees bent and place the LumbAtube™ or half-rolled towel under the largest arch of lower back.
- Raise both arms towards the ceiling holding a weighted object such as a Rebound Medicine Ball.
- Breathing in, slowly lower the arms overhead in an arch motion, resisting any arching of the lower back.
- As you reach the end phase of arm motion, forcefully breathe out through pursed lips, maintaining a strong abdominal brace, and slowly raise arms upwards towards the ceiling.

Note: *This exercise introduces coordination between the upper and mid body regions using a weighted object. This extended lever increases the intensity placed on abdominal bracing and effort required to maintain a strong neutral spine position.*

Single Leg Raise

To develop good coordination between the abdominal region and lower body as well as challenging the abdominal brace position a series of leg coordination exercises can be performed lying, sitting and standing.

INSTRUCTION

- Lie on back with arms by side and legs bent.
- Raise one leg from ground up to a 90-degree hip angle whilst maintaining strong abdominal brace and stable pelvis.
- Slowly, (count of 3) lower leg back to the ground.
- Repeat movement with opposite leg.

Fitness Ball Knee Lifts

Target Area –
Abdominal
brace whilst
raising leg
(balance &
coordination)

INSTRUCTION

- Sitting tall on the Fitness Ball, place feet shoulder-width apart and hands on hips.
- Draw stomach in and hold – maintaining a neutral spine.
- With strong left foot placement breathe in and slowly raise right knee up and hold, without leaning to the side.
- After holding for a count of 3 at the end position, slowly lower the leg and foot back to the starting position. Avoid moving feet.
- Repeat with opposite leg.
- Extend the leg after lifting the knee to increase the exercise intensity.

Note: *Keep movements slow and controlled with emphasis on small body and muscle adjustments. Focus on maintaining a stable pelvic position without twisting or leaning forward, backward or sideways or adjusting the foot position. This is achieved via a strong abdominal brace.*

Heel Slide

INSTRUCTION

- Lie on your back with knees bent and place the LumbAtube™ or half-rolled towel under the largest arch of lower back for support.
- Resting on your heels, forcefully breathe out through pursed lips whilst slowly extending the right heel along the ground until leg is fully extended.
- Breathing in, slowly reverse the action, drawing the heel back towards the body, resisting any arching of the lower back.
- Repeat with left leg.

Note: *This exercise challenges the ability to maintain neutral spine position and abdominal brace. Focus on the smaller details and maintaining good form.*

Isometric Abdominal Exercises

Isometric exercises provide the stimulus for effective neuromuscular development. A muscle held under static tension provides a building block for igniting a strong mind-body relationship for greater muscular control. Most importantly, isometric abdominal exercises aim to help protect the lower back. It is therefore important that good posture be maintained with minimal stress or load placed onto the lower back region. Any tension or pain to this area generally means the exercise is being performed incorrectly or a loss of abdominal contraction has occurred, in which case stop the exercise, readjust or rest before continuing without tension or pain.

The following isometric exercises aim to target the abdominal and lower back muscles in different positions. These exercises form the foundation for static strength in all planes of movement. The angle and position also challenge specific muscles and joints. Maintaining focus on the finer details of posture and making the necessary postural adjustments whilst holding an isometric position is important towards building a strong neuromuscular control. Each position can be held from 5-90 seconds or more, depending on one's current strength and ability level.

Good body posture from head-to-toe should also be considered when performing each exercise. Adapting the efficiency of a dancer with the strength of a gymnast provides a good visual approach to apply. Focusing on the quality of movement as opposed to quantity helps promote improvement. Once the quality is obtained the quantity element can be challenged.

The following 3 isometric subsections form part of isometric abdominal exercise training:

1. Front Support
2. Rear Support
3. Side Support

As the athlete learns to brace and breathe efficiently whilst performing isometric exercises, the challenge on the abdominal region can be increased through movement of the arms, legs or both. The movement of the limbs challenges the abdominal muscles even further by increasing the load through changes in center of gravity.

The initial goal is to master the abdominal brace holding pattern whilst continuing to breathe deeply through a range of body positions and holding patterns. Be certain to master one level of strength before progressing to the next. Exercises progress through basic isometric abdominal holds to more challenging positions where the abdominal region is braced yet movement of the arms or legs may be occurring – for example – performing a push-up. The challenge occurs in being able to hold the abdominal brace until fatigue sets in local muscles of the arms. This means the arms fatigue before the lower back starts to sag or the abdominal contraction is lost.

Level 1: Front Support

Level 2: Front Support – Toes Pointed

Level 3: Front Support – One Leg Raised

INSTRUCTION

- Rise up onto toes and hands and lean shoulders and body forward to ensure line of sight is ahead fingers.
- Brace abdominal muscles and ensure neutral spine position is established.
- Hold strong body position as you continue to breathe deeply in and out.

TIP: Hold this position for short periods of time (i.e. 10-60 seconds or more) or until the athlete loses form. Regular small body readjustments are required to maintain good body alignment.

Progression: Perform push-ups to challenge holding a tight body position.

Front Support Holds – on Forearms

INSTRUCTION

- Start in a Front Support position, resting on elbows and forearms with clenched fists on the ground.
- Lean the body forward until line of sight is over clenched fists. This ensures strong shoulder position and strong abdominal brace.
- Hold front support position breathing deeply in and out for a set period of time without losing abdominal brace or loss of body position.

Note: *Maintain strong abdominal brace. To increase the challenge, one leg can be raised and held a few inches whilst maintaining a strong core. Do not allow hips to tilt or any stress to radiate to the lower back region.*

THE BODY COACH

Body-Dish

Start

Midpoint

INSTRUCTION

- Lie on your back in an extended body position – legs together, toes pointed, arms overhead, hands together.
- Rise into a body dish position by simultaneously raising the arms and legs and drawing the lower back into the floor.
- Hold tight body position for a set period of time such as: 5–10 seconds or more.
- Ensure deep breathing is maintained whilst holding Body dish position.

Note: *To ensure good form is held, beginners may start with one leg bent and foot on the ground and the other leg extended with toes pointed – raising just one leg with the arms into body dish position. (This decreases the load and allows progression.)*

Variation:
1. *Repetitions: Perform a series of dish hold repetitions, raising and lowering for short periods (i.e. 2 seconds and then repeat)*
2. *Body Dish Rolls: Maintain long body position and complete single body rolls to the left, from back to side, side to front, front to side and then back onto your back. Repeat rolls back to the left side.*

12 Rear Support Holds

Start Position

Raise and Hold

INSTRUCTION

- Lie on your back with your knees bent and arms by your side.
- Slowly raise hips off ground and gently peel one vertebra at a time, using your abdominals, off the mat to 'ski-jump' position (knees, hips and shoulders in a similar line).
- Complete up to 5 breathing cycles. Maintain the position, keeping the pelvic floor lifted and the abdominals braced.
- Exhale as you gently lower the body to the ground.

Note: *A more advanced version can be performed with the feet raised on a fitness ball.*

The Hundred Drill

13

Beginner

Intermediate

Advanced
Pulse arms up to 100 times

INSTRUCTION

- Lie on your back in an extended position. Raise legs whilst maintaining a strong abdominal brace position and inhale to prepare.
- Exhale as you curl upper body and raise head – ribs drawn to the hips and navel drawn to the spine. Arms at side are raised approximately 3 inches from the floor, palms facing downwards.
- Inhale for 5 arm pumps and exhale 5 pumps as in the previous level until you have reached 100 or 10 breath cycles.
- Maintain the head and neck in neutral spine position, without tension.

14 Side Supports – Collins Lateral Hold

INSTRUCTION

- Lie on side with upper body supported by the elbow (90 degrees, directly below shoulder), forearm and clenched fist.
- Lift the pelvis off the ground, eliminating the side bending by raising onto the edge of feet, forming a straight line from the feet to head – maintaining a neutral position.
- Maintain a strong abdominal brace and breathe deeply.
- Rise up and hold body position for 3–5 breathing cycles – left side, then repeat right side.

Note: *Legs can be crossed in front of the body to reduce the load.*

15 Side Supports – Leg Raised

Note: *Raise leg to increase exercise intensity.*

THE BODY COACH

Raise Arm

Lower Arm

Note: *In Side Support position raise and lower arm (with or without hand weight) to challenge the abdominal brace position and center of gravity. See exercise 14 for description.*

Add light hand weight to increase exercise intensity (see exercise 45).

Muscle Endurance

Once a good isometric hold can be maintained, muscle endurance exercises are introduced targeting four key muscle regions. Generally all muscles are involved in one form or another in each exercise. With some drill modification though, you can shift the major emphasis from one region to another or one muscle to another at a higher intensity. For example, the upper and lower abdominal region is one muscle group, although a higher emphasis is placed on the upper fibers when performing a movement from the upper region downwards – curling exercise.

The upper abdominal muscles fire with both lower abdominal and oblique exercises. On the other hand, the lower portion has a higher activation when the legs are used or lifting occurs from the lower region upwards, for example, with reverse curls. Since the lower back and abdominal muscles play a dominant role in controlling posture, exercises for this region are included. Each exercise is associated with a particular movement pattern that targets the following 4 regions:

1. **Upper abdominal fibers:** Upper portion of rectus abdominus worked through a range of motion of up to 30 degrees (see angle on page 41)

2. **Abdominal obliques:** Internal and external obliques

3. **Lower abdominal fibers:** Lower portion of rectus abdominus as well as deeper transversus abdominus muscles

4. **Lower back:** Muscles of the lower back region

Lower Back Support

The Body Coach® LumbAtube™ or half-rolled towel is used to help support the lower back in performing various abdominal exercises. These exercises can be performed with or without this assistance. Many exercises that follow demonstrate this lower back support being used.

Levers – Controlling the Exercise Intensity

A lever is the length and angle of a muscle or pair of muscles from a joint. The further the limbs are extended away from a point of stress (increasing angle of joint) the higher the intensity of the exercise, especially when working against gravity. Yet, if we shorten the lever by bending a muscle group and/or its joints we reduce the intensity or load.

Progressing in activities of a short lever nature towards a longer lever movement with good form will allow proper and effective strengthening of the abdominal muscles. In most cases it is simply a matter of changing the arm or leg position to increase the exercise intensity, as shown in the abdominal curl exercise below.

Short Lever – Lower Intensity

Long Lever – Higher Intensity

UPPER ABDOMINAL FIBERS

Abdominal Slide

Hands on Thighs

Slide Palms of Hands to Knees

INSTRUCTION

- Lie on your back with knees bent and place the LumbAtube™ or a half-rolled towel under the largest arch of lower back and rest hands on thighs.
- Breathing in through the nose, then out through the mouth with pursed lips draw your naval (belly button) inwards and hold – bracing the abdominal muscles.
- Maintaining a strong abdominal brace, forcefully breathe out through pursed lips, whilst sliding hands up thighs for a count of three until palms reach the knees.
- Breathe in as you lower for a count of three.

Abdominal Crunch – Levers

Level 1: Short Lever – Lower Intensity

Level 2: Mid Lever – Moderate Intensity

Level 3: Long Lever – Higher Intensity

INSTRUCTION

- Lie on your back with knees bent and place the LumbAtube™ or a half-rolled towel under the largest arch of lower back and rest hands on thighs.
  Level 1: Fold arms across chest
  Level 2: Touch hands behind head
  Level 3: Extend arms overhead
- Maintaining a strong abdominal brace, forcefully breathe out through pursed lips, whilst crunching abdominal muscles bringing your sternum towards hips, then lower.

Lowered

Raised

INSTRUCTION

- Lie on your back with knees bent and feet shoulder width apart.
- Extend arms above waistline, fists together.
- Maintaining a strong abdominal brace, forcefully breathe out through pursed lips, whilst extending hands between legs ready to rise like a water-skier for a count of three.
- Breathe in as you lower for a count of three.

Note: *Place the LumbAtube™ or a half-rolled towel under the largest arch of lower back for support.*

Lowered

Raised

INSTRUCTION

- Lie on your back with legs raised from hip at 90-degrees and slightly bent.

- Place hands behind head.

- Breathing out, raise shoulders off the ground bringing sternum towards pelvis, then lower.

- Avoid swinging legs or taking hip angle beyond 90 degrees due to the stress placed on the lower back region.

Lowered

Raised

INSTRUCTION

- Lie on your back with legs raised from hip at 90-degrees and slightly bent.

- Extend arms up above eye line.

- Breathing out, raise shoulders off the ground and reach hands up towards feet, then lower.

- Avoid swinging legs or taking hip angle beyond 90 degrees due to the stress placed on the lower back region.

 **Level 1:** Arms Forward

 **Level 2:** Arms Across Chest

 **Level 3:** Arms Overhead

INSTRUCTION

- Lie on ball on arch of back, legs bent and feet shoulder width apart.
  Level 1: Extend arms forward at 90-degree angle to chest
  Level 2: Fold arms across chest
  Level 3: Extend arms overhead
- Contracting the abdominal muscles and breathing out, slowly crunch and curl the stomach muscles up (similar to a banana shape), without moving the hips or rolling on the ball, then lower – breathing in.
- Maintain the head in its neutral position throughout to avoid neck tension.

Lowered

Raised

INSTRUCTIONS

- Lie on your back with knees bent and place the LumbAtube™ or a half-rolled towel under the largest arch of lower back whilst resting on your heels.
- Extend arms overhead.
- Maintaining a strong abdominal brace, forcefully breath out through pursed lips, whilst simultaneously raising right leg (bent) and both arms towards each other.
- Then lower, breathing in. Repeat with left leg and both arms.

Note: *This exercise introduces coordination between the upper, mid and lower body regions.*

ABDOMINAL OBLIQUES

24 Lateral Side Raises

Lowered

Raised

INSTRUCTION

- Lie on your side, legs extended, toes pointed and feet together.
- The arm closest to the ground extends above head with palm facing towards ceiling – head relaxed resting on inner part of arm.
- The upper arm is bent, supporting your body weight in front of the body.
- Breathing in through the nose, then out through the mouth with pursed lips draw your naval (belly button) inwards and hold – maintaining a neutral spine.
- Maintaining a long body position, forcefully breathe out through pursed lips and simultaneously raise legs and arm into the air, then lower.
- Repeat on opposite side.

Chest Cross-overs

Level 1: Arms Folded Across Chest

Level 2: Arms Behind Head

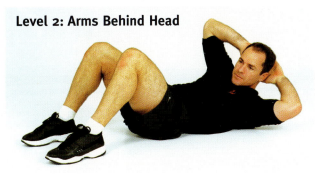

INSTRUCTION

- Lie on your back with your knees bent:
  Level 1: Arms folded across chest
  Level 2: Arms behind head
- Draw your stomach inwards and hold – bracing the abdominal muscles.
- Focus attention on raising one shoulder up and across towards the opposite knee, then lower.
- Repeat action on opposite side.

INSTRUCTION

- Lie on your back with legs raised from hip at 90-degrees and slightly bent.
- Place right arm by your side and the left arm raised into the air.
- Breathing out, raise left shoulder off the ground reaching hand towards foot, then lower. Repeat.
- Avoid swinging legs or taking hip angle beyond 90 degrees due to the stress placed on the lower back region.
- Repeat action using right arm.

Extended Starting Position

Elbow to Knee Action

INSTRUCTION

- Lie on your back with right leg straight and raised off the ground in an extended position.
- Place your left arm behind your head and your right arm by your side.
- Draw your stomach inwards and hold – bracing the abdominal muscles.
- Use LumbAtube™ or half-rolled towel to support the lower back, if necessary.
- Simultaneously raise the left shoulder and bring right knee in towards left elbow, then lower.
- Repeat action on opposite side bringing right elbow to left knee.

Slowly Lower Body Eccentrically to Ground

INSTRUCTION

- Lie on your back with knees bent and hands behind head.
- Place LumbAtube™ or a half-rolled towel under the largest arch of lower back for support, if necessary.
- Maintaining a strong abdominal brace, forcefully breathe out through pursed lips, whilst crunching abdominal muscles.
- Raise shoulders above normal height of 30-degree angle and hold briefly.
- Slowly lower for a count of three to five seconds.
- Repeat action.

Twist from Knee-to-knee

INSTRUCTION

- Sit up at 45-60 degree angle with legs slightly bent and arms extended forwards holding medicine ball.
- Keeping the abdominals braced and shoulders square move the medicine ball from side to side – outside the line of knee – using the arms only.
- Maintain a deep breathing pattern throughout.

Note: *This movement uses primarily the arms and limits any body rotation or lower back twisting to avoid injury.*

Start Position

Midpoint

INSTRUCTION

- Lie on your back with hands behind your head and knees raised into table top position (90-degrees at hip and knees in air).
- Simultaneously raise left shoulder and elbow and bend right knee in towards left elbow, then lower.
- Reset your body in start position to ensure proper movement.
- Repeat action with right shoulder and left leg.
- Aim to keep the pelvis still and feel like you are wringing out a wet cloth.

Fitness Ball Oblique Twist

INSTRUCTION

- Lie on fitness ball at shoulder height with hips raised and body parallel to ground.
- Feet shoulder-width apart, arms extended above chest, hands together.
- Contract the abdominal region as you slowly twist the body, lower the arms to the left side – simultaneously bending at the knee and rotating the hip, torso and shoulders across the ball until arms are parallel to ground.
- Keeping arms extended, rotate across the ball to the right side.
- The fitness ball moves underneath your body as your shoulders twist.
- Rise onto shoulder region on ball.
- Move head in time with body and in line with shoulder in neutral position. Rotate slowly under tension for a count of 3 to each side.
- Add weight to hands (i.e. medicine ball) to increase intensity.

LOWER ABDOMINAL FIBERS

32 Single Leg Stretch

INSTRUCTION

- Lie flat on your back with both knees raised at a 90-degree angle.
- Place hands behind back of knee for support.
- Maintaining a strong abdominal brace, extend one leg and draw the other leg in – catching bent leg with both hands.
- Repeat action with opposite leg.

Note: *To increase the activation of the abdominal muscles, raise the head and shoulders off the ground whilst performing this exercise. Keep the ribs drawn to the hips and the navel to the spine, stabilizing the torso as you work on lengthening the legs.*

THE BODY COACH

INSTRUCTION

- Lie flat on your back with your knees bent and arms resting on your chest.
- Maintaining a strong abdominal brace and neutral spine position, simultaneously draw lower abdominal muscles in and raise one leg up until thigh is vertical, then slowly lower.
- Repeat with opposite leg.
- Straighten leg to increase intensity of exercise.

Note: *To maximize the use of the lower abdominal muscles focus on maintaining a good abdominal brace and neutral spine position whilst raising and lowering the leg for a count of three seconds each. Initiate movement via lower abdominal muscle fibers.*

34 Reverse Curl

INSTRUCTION

- Lie flat on your back with your knees bent and arms by your side.
- Place LumbAtube™ or small rolled towel between your thighs and squeeze legs together.
- Maintaining a strong abdominal brace and neutral spine position, simultaneously draw lower abdominal muscles in and raise legs up together until buttocks lift off ground, then slowly lower.
- Increase lift action from pelvic region once abdominal muscles become stronger.

Note: *To maximize the use of the lower abdominal muscles avoid swinging the legs and maintain a good abdominal brace and neutral spine position by initiating movement via the lower abdominal muscle fibers.*

Lower Leg Lifts

Start Position

Raised

INSTRUCTION

- Lie on your back with legs raised in the air and slightly bent and hands placed under your buttocks – palms facing down.
- Place LumbAtube™ or half-rolled towel under neck for support, if necessary.
- Maintaining a strong abdominal brace, activate the lower abdominal region and raise legs into the air without swinging legs or changing their length.
- Over time, with good abdominal contraction you will learn to relax the upper body and focus on solely activating the abdominal region.

Note: *To increase the intensity of this exercise, lie on an exercise bench – holding the end of the bench with both hands and raised legs into the air. A twist (corkscrew) action of the legs can also be added when raising once good core-strength is obtained to also strengthen the obliques.*

Start Position

**Raise Head
Off Ground and
Swap Legs**

INSTRUCTION

- Lie flat on back.
- Exhale as you contract your abdominal muscles by drawing your ribs to your hips, your navel to your spine and extend one leg towards ceiling at a 90-degree angle to your body – toes pointed.
- Release one leg, toes pointed, and lower to approximately six-inches off the ground and pulse for a count of 3 whilst bracing the other leg with both hands.
- Return leg to upright position and repeat with opposite leg.

LOWER BACK

Hip Raise

Start Position

Raised

INSTRUCTION

- Lie on your back with your knees bent and arms by your side.
- Exhale as you gently peel one vertebra up at a time, using your abdominals up to a ramp type position (knees, hips and shoulders in a similar line).
- Maintain this position, keeping the pelvic floor lifted and the abdominals braced.
- Exhale as you gently imprint one vertebra at a time, using your abdominals back to the mat, keeping weight distribution even in the feet.

Controlled Back Raise

Start Position

Raised

INSTRUCTION

- Lie on stomach with hands gently clasped behind back.
- Gently brace abdominal muscles.
- Breathing in, slowly raise upper body (chest) off floor.
- Focus on elongating the spine and rising away and up a short distance whilst maintaining braced abdominal muscles.
- Breathing out, slowly lower the body to the floor.

Note: *Focus on the activation of the lower back muscles.*

Supermans

Start Position

Raised

INSTRUCTION

- Lie face down with arms and legs extended.
- Inhale as you lift right arm and left leg off floor. Avoid arching or twisting your spine.
- Exhale as you lower right arm and left leg and lift left arm and right leg. Begin the exercise slowly, in a controlled manner.
- Inhale for 3 movements and exhale for 3 movements.
- Do not hold or stop movement, nor let your feet or arms touch the ground. Stabilize the torso, focus on length as opposed to height and keep the shoulders away from the ears.

4-Point Kneeling – Alternate Arm and Leg Raise

Start Position on All Fours

Arm and Leg Raised Simultaneously

INSTRUCTION

- Kneel on knees and hands and create an equal equilibrium between all 4 points.
- Maintaining a strong abdominal brace and neutral spine position, forcefully breathe out through pursed lips whilst simultaneously extending one leg backwards, with knee slightly flexed, and the opposite arm forward.
- Resisting any arching of the lower back or neck, breathe in and bring leg and arm back to starting position.
- Repeat movement opposite side.

Note: *Minimize any movement of the body apart from arms and legs.*

Lie over Fitness Ball

Raise until Body is Inline

INSTRUCTION

- Lie on fitness ball on stomach, with knees shoulder-width apart, arms bent, fingers resting against side of head.
- Keeping the body extended, raise the chest off the ball until a straight line is formed between the legs and upper body and then lower.
- Perform movement slowly and controlled keeping abdominal muscles braced.

**Start Position
on All Fours
over Ball**

**Arm and
Leg Raised
Simulateneously**

INSTRUCTION

- Lie on fitness ball with equal weight on feet and hands on the ground to create an equilibrium between all 4 points.
- Maintaining a strong abdominal brace and neutral spine position, forcefully breathe out through pursed lips whilst simultaneously extending one leg up off the ground until parallel and the opposite arm forward.
- Resisting any arching of the lower back or neck, breathe in and bring leg and arm back to starting position.
- Repeat movement on opposite side.

Note: *Minimize any movement of the body apart from arms and legs.*

Strength and Motor Coordination

Motor coordination patterns are the building blocks to more complex skills. Movement of the arms and legs only makes it more difficult to sustain a solid abdominal contraction. Mastering Phases 1–3 provides the foundation for effective strength gains to occur. Phase 4 now provides the training stimulus for increased strength gains. An important element in strength training is making a conscious effort to keep a constant state of tension on your abdominal muscles throughout the movement. By simply varying a body angle or position, in some exercises the weight of your upper or lower extremity will be enough to produce the demand on the muscle. Other exercises may require overloading through the introduction of a weighted implement such as a medicine ball, dumbbell or machine. Either way for optimal increases in strength to occur, muscular fatigue should occur with low repetitions between 8–12 repetitions with each rep taking between 2–4 seconds to complete. Performing lower back strengthening exercises is also required for muscular balance as well as strength for deceleration and controlling high speed forward flexion and rotation found in Phase 5.

The following exercises focus on strength and motor coordination for the abdominal muscles and lower back region.

Fitness Ball Walk-out

Midpoint

Start Position

Endpoint

INSTRUCTION

- Lie on ball on stomach with hands and feet on the ground.
- Slowly roll forward onto hands and brace abdominal muscles.
- Maintain deep breathing pattern whilst walking hands forward.
- Keep abdominal muscles tight and lifted as the ball reaches the legs and works towards the feet.
- Resist any arching or sagging of the lower back as the body lever becomes longer.
- Hold briefly at endpoint in front support position and return to starting position maintaining control of your body and the ball until you rest at the starting position.

Note: *Maintain strong abdominal brace and neutral spine position when walking body out away from fitness ball. Beginners start by walking out to the thighs only. As strength improves, progress out to the ankles avoiding any lower back sagging and perform a push-up. Ensure head and neck alignment is maintained at all times with the rest of the body for the development of good posture.*

Start Position

Midpoint

INSTRUCTION

- Start in front support position with feet on ball and hands on ground.
  Level 1: Shin or ankle (point toes)
  Level 2: Up on toes (as shown)
- Maintaining strong abdominal brace and good body position, roll ball forwards towards chest by bending knees, then outwards to starting position.
- Continually readjust stomach, head and neck alignment and hip position to ensure neutral spine position is maintained.
- Breathe out when extending legs back.
- Breath in when bringing knees to chest.

Front Support – on Hands

Midrange

Plank – on Forearms

- Starting in a front support position with the lower extremities:

  (a) Beginner – Resting on knees and hands
  (b) Advanced – Resting on toes and hands

- Hold this front support whilst adjusting neutral spine position.

- Breathing-in lower onto to one forearm.

- Keep the hips square (avoid any rotation of the pelvis) then onto the other forearm and hold this position (the Plank position).

- Breath-out in Plank position – raise on one hand then up onto the other in front support position to complete one repetition.

- Repeat sequence up and down.

- Vary from left to right arms when lowering and raising body.

Note: *Perform movement continuously up and down without twisting, tilting or waddling of the hips for set amount of reps or until loss of form. Maintain strong shoulder and abdominal positions throughout exercise.*

Ensure head and neck alignment is maintained at all times with the rest of the body for the development of good posture.

Collins Lateral Fly™ (Weighted)

Raised Arm

Lower Arm

INSTRUCTION

- Rise up onto forearm directly under shoulder with body in straight line resting on feet.
- Extend arm forward of the body with weight in hand.
- Raise and lower the arm up and down to challenge one's center of gravity and abdominal oblique muscles.
- Maintain strong abdominal brace, deep breathing pattern and straight body alignment with movement of the arm.
- Repeat on opposite side with opposite arm.

Fitness Ball Roll-outs

Start Position

Midpoint

INSTRUCTION

- Kneel on ground with body angled at 45 degrees – fists clenched resting side-by-side on fitness ball.
- Keeping the body tight, slowly roll the ball forward, raising the pelvis and knees and positioning the upper body parallel to the ground.
- Rest on forearms and toes, with feet shoulder-width apart, then return to starting position.
- Maintain strong arm, shoulder, abdominal and lower back positioning.

Note: *To increase intensity, bring feet close together or raise one leg slightly off the ground.*

Weighted Toe Touches

Lowered

Raised

INSTRUCTION

- Lie on your back with legs raised from hip at 90-degrees and slightly bent.
- Extend arms up above eye line holding medicine ball.
- Breathing out, raise shoulders off the ground and reach medicine ball up towards feet, then lower.
- Avoid swinging legs or taking hip angle beyond 90 degrees due to the stress placed on the lower back region.

Overhead Weighted Toe Touches

Lowered   **Raised**

INSTRUCTION

- Lie on your back with legs raised from hip at 90-degrees and slightly bent.
- Extend arms overhead and rest on ground holding medicine ball in both hands.
- Breathing out, simultaneously raise medicine ball, arms and shoulders off the ground by crunching the abdominal region.
- Reach up for the toes, then slowly lower to starting position always remaining in control.

Start Position

Midpoint

INSTRUCTION

- Lie on your back with legs bent and arms extended overhead holding medicine ball.
- Brace the abdominal muscles.
- Breathing out, simultaneously raise the arms, shoulders and one leg to meet at a midpoint and then lower.
- Repeat movement using opposite leg.

Elbow to Knee (Weighted)

Start Position

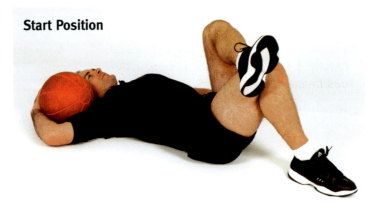

Midpoint

INSTRUCTION

- Lie on your back with medicine ball grasped on right shoulder and left leg resting across the right knee.
- Gently brace the abdominal muscles and hold.
- Focus attention on raising one shoulder up and across towards the opposite knee, then lower.
- Repeat action on opposite side.

LOWER ABDOMINAL SEQUENCE

Captains Chair Exercises

Position: Rest forearms on pads, grip handles and brace abdominal muscles with the lower back supported by backing pad. Extend legs slightly forwards to activate abdominal and iliopsoas muscles.

Knee Raises

INSTRUCTION

- Maintaining a strong abdominal brace, breathe out and slowly raise knees to chest, then lower.
- Avoid legs swinging or lower back arching.
- Ensure lower back is held firmly against backing pad at all times by maintaining strong abdominal brace.

Obliques Twist

Start Position

Midpoint

INSTRUCTION

- Slowly raise knees up and across towards one shoulder, then lower extending the legs down.
- Repeat action raising knees across to opposite shoulder.
- Ensure lower back is held firmly against backing pad at all times by maintaining strong abdominal brace.

Scissors

Start Position

Midpoint

INSTRUCTION

- Slowly raise one leg up until parallel to the ground, then lower.
- Repeat action with opposite leg.
- Ensure lower back is held firmly against backing pad at all times by maintaining strong abdominal brace.

Parallel Holds

Start Position

Midpoint

INSTRUCTION

- Maintaining a strong abdominal brace raise both legs up until parallel to the ground and hold – toes pointed.
- Ensure lower back is held firmly against backing pad at all times to reduce any chance of lower back arching.
- Maintain deep breathing pattern until loss of form, then lower legs whether after 1 second or 30 seconds.
- Focus on exercise quality and correct body position.

Hanging Knee/Leg Raises

Start Position  **Midpoint**

INSTRUCTION

- Grip an overhead bar with wide grip.
- Keep legs slightly bent and brace abdominal muscles.
- Level 1: Breathing out, raise knees up to chest, then lower legs slowly (see Test 4, page 106).
- Level 2: Breathing out, raise feet up to overhead bar, then lower legs slowly (as shown).
- Aim to maintain a tight body position at all times and avoid abdominal swinging (weakness).

Note: *A spotter may be necessary to support the lower back region of the participant to avoid swinging of the body. Remember, all exercises are based on progression of intensity and should not be attempted until a good strength base is obtained.*

Dumbbell Front Raise

Start Position

Midpoint

INSTRUCTION

- Grip dumbbell in both hands (as shown) and brace abdominal muscles.
- Start by slightly bending the knees in a quarter squat position and holding the dumbbell with straight arms at groin height.
- Maintaining straight arms, raise dumbbell in arc motion in front of body up to eye level whilst straightening legs.
- Slowly lower arms and weight ensuring abdominal muscles remain braced.
- Repeat action with good form.

Cable Crunches

Start Position

Midpoint

INSTRUCTION

- Kneel on ground in front of overhead cable machine.
- Grasp triceps rope with both hands and place in front of forehead whilst keeping back flat.
- Crunch the abdominal muscles down to midpoint, keeping the hips and legs fixed and then return slowly up to starting point.
- Maintain good body position and use weight that allows proper form.

Variation: *To focus on the obliques, lower with a twist to one side.*

Abdominal Crunch Machine

Start Position

Midpoint

INSTRUCTION

- Sit in abdominal crunch machine and make appropriate adjustments to suit your height and body position.
- Establish suitable weight load of exercise.
- Place arms across chest pad and grip handles.
- Breathing out, crunch abdominal muscles down against resistance and then slowly allow pad to return to upright position.
- Maintain good body position and use weight that allows proper form.

Note: *All abdominal crunch machines will vary in their shape, design and function – adjust accordingly.*

Start Position

Midpoint

INSTRUCTION

- Sit in rotary oblique machine and make appropriate adjustments to suit your height, leg and arm position.
- Raise arms against pad and grip handles with both hands.
- Establish suitable weight load of exercise.
- Activating the abdominal oblique muscles, breathe out and slowly rotate torso to the left side and then back to starting point.
- Complete set and then adjust machine to rotate to the right side.

Note: *All rotary oblique machines will vary in their shape, design and function – adjust accordingly.*

Lower Back Extension

Start Position

Midpoint

INSTRUCTION

- Set adjustment height of foot pads to suit body position.
- Holding onto handles, lean body forward across hip and thigh pad with heels positioned under foot pads.
- Bend at hip and lean down with arms crossed in front of chest.
- Breathing out, slowly raise the body up from the waist until body is in one line, then slowly lower while breathing in.
- To increase the intensity of the exercise, hold a weight plate across the chest.

Note: *All lower back extension machines will vary in their shape, design and function – adjust accordingly.*

Power
Development

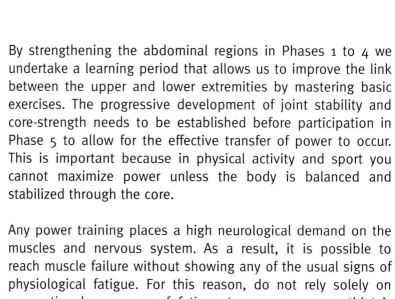

By strengthening the abdominal regions in Phases 1 to 4 we undertake a learning period that allows us to improve the link between the upper and lower extremities by mastering basic exercises. The progressive development of joint stability and core-strength needs to be established before participation in Phase 5 to allow for the effective transfer of power to occur. This is important because in physical activity and sport you cannot maximize power unless the body is balanced and stabilized through the core.

Any power training places a high neurological demand on the muscles and nervous system. As a result, it is possible to reach muscle failure without showing any of the usual signs of physiological fatigue. For this reason, do not rely solely on conventional measures of fatigue to measure your athlete's recovery rate. As more powerful exercises are introduced in Phase 5 up to 180 seconds rest is recommended between sets.

Phase 5 requires exercise discipline, as the quality of movement is more beneficial than quantity of exercise repetitions or sets. Therefore, always maintain good technique, as once good posture or form is lost, the exercise should be stopped immediately and a recovery period undertaken. The weight of the medicine ball being used in various exercises will depend on the athlete's training age and core-strength ability. Having a selection of sizes available will enable you to modify intensity accordingly for strength, speed or power applications.

The following exercises are used to improve abdominal power development.

Overhead

Release Point

INSTRUCTION

- In a large open area, stand tall, brace abdominals and extend medicine ball above head with arms straight.
- Bend arms and lower medicine ball behind head.
- Simultaneously step forward with one leg, 'crunch' abdominal muscles and thrust arms forwards releasing medicine ball.
- Ensure crunch action from sternum to pelvis occurs for appropriate abdominal power development.
- Chase ball, trap and repeat.

INSTRUCTION

- Stand tall, brace abdominals and extend medicine ball overhead with arms straight.
- Simultaneously jump as you thrust medicine ball downwards and crunch abdominal muscles.
- Bend legs slightly to absorb shock through body.
- Catch ball and repeat.

Variation: *Perform single or multiple repetitions with or without jumping.*

Medicine Ball Squat Release

Squat

Release

INSTRUCTION

- Find clear open space such as a sports oval.
- Stand in upright position with feet shoulder width apart and medicine ball held at chest height.
- Breathing in, slowly lower into a squat position.
- Breathing out, explode up onto the toes pushing the medicine ball up and forwards as far as possible maintaining good form.

Variation: *Stand 2-5 meters away from a solid, concrete wall. Squat, release ball to wall and catch (concentric/eccentric loading) and repeat.*

65

Power Jumps

INSTRUCTION

- Stand with medicine ball between feet and tighten grip.
- Breathe in deeply and then breathe out and explode the feet up into the air bringing the knees towards the chest.
- As the feet and knees raise, release the medicine ball up into the air in front of the body and then catch the ball and land absorbing the shock by bending the knees and bracing the abdominal muscles.
- Reset and repeat.

Variation: *Throw ball back behind the body using leg curl motion.*

INSTRUCTION

A: Release (concentric thrust)
- Stand with feet shoulder-width apart with medicine ball in hand to side of body in open area (ie. sports field).
- Brace abdominal muscles and thrust ball across the body and release whilst rotating feet.
- Retrieve medicine ball or work with partner.
- Repeat thrust on opposite side of body.

B: Release and Catch (concentric and eccentric)
- Stand sideways to a concrete wall or partner approximately 3–5 meters away.
- Brace abdominal muscles and thrust ball across the body and release whilst rotating feet and arms.
- Allow ball to hit wall then bounce back on ground before catching or have it caught by partner and thrust back.
- Repeat thrust on opposite side of body.

Cross Opposite Elbow to Opposite Knee

INSTRUCTION

- Stand tall with both arms bent and clenched fist raised at eye level.
- Brace abdominal muscles and hold chest tall.
- Start by marching on the spot and raising knees tall whilst rotating opposite elbow to knee.
- Look forward with chest held tall and head in neutral position.
- Gradually increase speed of exercise into a stationary skip and then move forwards.
- Maintain quality of movement with emphasis on strong abdominal brace, deep breathing pattern and good body position.

INSTRUCTION

- Face your partner in a front support position 1–2 meters apart.
- Brace abdominal muscles and hold position.
- Start with medicine ball in right hand and push across to partner – vary sides.
- The partner traps the ball with hand and simultaneously pushes the ball back across.
- Keep hips square and maintain a good front support body position.
- Reduce distance and increase speed of push as time progresses.

Medicine Ball Chest Push

Ready to Catch

Ready to Push

INSTRUCTION

- The athlete sits on the ground with hands raised whilst the coach stands with medicine ball at chest height approximately 1–3 meters away.
- The coach gently pushes the ball across to the athlete who catches it at chest height and simultaneously lowers down to the ground in a controlled manner with the ball on the chest.
- Upon reaching the ground the athlete raises forward and pushes the ball back to the coach who catches and repeats the action.
- Maintain strong abdominal brace and total body control throughout movement.

Variation: *For concentric only loading, thrust the ball up from the chest off the ground. The coach catches and then rolls the ball back to the athlete. For eccentric loading only, the coach throws the ball to the athlete who catches and rolls back to ground with ball on chest. The athlete then rolls the ball back to the coach.*

Medicine Ball Overhead Thrust

Ready to Catch

Ready to Thrust

INSTRUCTION

- The athlete sits on the ground with hands raised whilst the coach stands with medicine ball at chest height approximately 1–3 meters away.
- The coach gently pushes the ball across to the athlete who catches it at head height and simultaneously lowers down to the ground in a controlled manner with the ball taken overhead.
- Upon reaching the ground the athlete raises forward and thrusts the ball back to the coach who catches and repeats the action.
- Maintain strong abdominal brace and total body control throughout movement.

Variation: *For concentric only loading, thrust the ball up from overhead off the ground. The coach catches and then rolls the ball back to the athlete. For eccentric loading only, the coach throws the ball to the athlete who catches the ball and rolls back to ground with ball overhead. The athlete then rolls the ball back to the coach.*

Chapter 7

Testing Abdominal Strength

Testing abdominal strength plays a vital role in developing an athlete's overall development. It also helps assist coaches to understand what developmental level the athlete is currently positioned in terms of muscular strength and coordination. Assessing, identifying and recording athlete ability and potential also provides the coach with the appropriate data to design varied training sessions relating to the ability of the athlete, whilst also providing a benchmark for future reference. Testing abdominal strength can also provide direction and motivation to the athlete and vital feedback for the coach. Essentially all exercises can be used as a test of strength, muscle control and power.

The following abdominal tests provide a good base to work from.

TEST 1: BODY DISH

Start

Midpoint

INSTRUCTION:

- Lie on your back in an extended body position – legs together, toes pointed, arms overhead, hands together.
- Rise into a body dish position by simultaneously raising the arms and legs and drawing the lower back into the floor.
- Hold tight body position, whilst breathing deeply until fatigue or loss of form – whether 1 second or 60 seconds or more.
- This includes arm and shoulder position, leg position and any lower back arching.
- Record time held in seconds:
  Attempt 1: _____
  Attempt 2: _____

Body Dish Roll Test:
Using wide open clear space, aim to perform three (3) continuous rolls to the right aiming to keep a tight body position and straight rolling line. Repeat on the left side.

TEST 2: FRONT SUPPORT RAISE

Starting Position

Raised Position

INSTRUCTION

- Start in a front support position with eye line positioned over fingernails and abdominal muscles braced.
- Partner stands to the side of the legs in line with the knees gripping underneath either side of the knee.
- On go, the athlete contracts the muscles of the body as the partner slowly raises the athlete's legs into the air into a streamline body position.

Front Support Raise, continued:

- The athlete leans forward as the partner lifts so as to maintain a tight body position. (i.e. Keep body weight forward over hands.)
- Hold the body in a straight line (without sagging) for a set period of time or until loss of form. The athlete should never feel pain or arch the lower back, if so **STOP** and lower.
- Maintain a deep breathing pattern throughout. Never hold the breath.
- Ensure the head remains forward of the hands.
- Lower the athlete slowly to the ground. The athlete should maintain a tight body position until the partner releases the legs once on the ground.
- As the athlete becomes stronger, the test can be performed by lifting the body from the ankles.
- Record time held with proper body position.

Note: *It is important for the person lifting to assess the athlete's lower back for sagging whilst lifting – a sign of weakness. If so, 'stop' and lower the athlete, readjust and start again ensuring a strong abdominal brace is held. Shorten the lever length to decrease the possibility of lower back arching (i.e. lift from the knees, not the ankles). Stop the exercise once arching occurs.*

TEST 3: ABDOMINAL SLIDE

Hands on Thighs

Slide Palms of Hands to Knees

INSTRUCTION

- Lie on your back with knees bent and place the LumbAtube™ or a half-rolled towel under the largest arch of lower back and rest hands on thighs.
- Maintaining a strong abdominal brace, slide hands up thighs until palms reach the knees. Breathe in as you lower your back to the ground.
- Record score for 30 or 60 seconds completing full abdominal slide up and down to complete 1 repetition.

Note: *Maintain a neutral head and neck position with the body throughout the exercise. Avoid stooping the head forward when rising up – this is a sign of poor body awareness and weak neck and abdominal muscles.*

TEST 4: HANGING KNEE RAISES

INSTRUCTION

- Grip an overhead bar with a wide grip.
- Keep legs slightly bent and brace abdominal muscles.
- Breathing out, raise knees up to chest, then lower legs slowly.
- Aim to maintain a tight body position at all times and avoid abdominal swinging (weakness).
- Count total number of repetitions performed correctly.

Note: *A spotter may be necessary to support the lower back region of the participant to avoid swinging.*

THE BODY COACH

Test Score Sheet

On the score sheet below record your test scores in time (seconds) or repetitions (Reps). After each exercise have the person testing you describe details about elements such as your posture, breathing, body position and movement pattern.

Initial Test Date:

Test	Report	Score
1. Body Dish	Total Time in secs	
Description		
2. Front Support Raise	Total Time in secs	
Description		
3. Abdominal Slide	Reps in 30 secs	
	Reps in 60 secs	
Description		
4. Hanging Knee Raises	Total Reps	
Description		

2nd Test Date:

Test	Report	Score
1. Body Dish	Total Time in secs	
Description		
2. Front Support Raise	Total Time in secs	
Description		
3. Abdominal Slide	Reps in 30 secs	
	Reps in 60 secs	
Description		
4. Hanging Knee Raises	Total Reps	
Description		

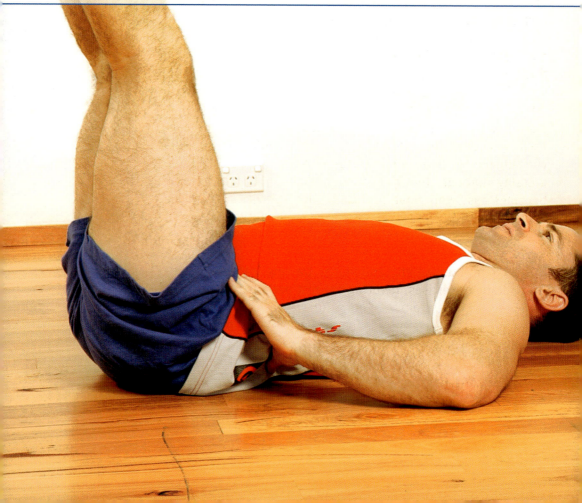

Chapter 8

Abdominal Exercise Routines

Routines are a great way to help establish a strong center of power in the body. An abdominal training routine supplements fitness and sports training by providing a system for gaining strength and protecting the lower back region. The abdominal region itself consists of a number of muscle groups that can be trained using the 5 specific phases described in this book. Every person will vary in his or her ability to perform the same exercise. What may be seen as easy for one-person may be be hard for another. As a result, the number of repetitions, sets and rest will need to be determined by a certified fitness professional or physio-therapist who will assess your technique.

Determining Repetitions and Sets

The ideal number of repetitions (reps) varies between 8-12 and 12-15 reps, for strength and endurance respectively, and 3 sets per exercise. As muscle needs to be overloaded to stimulate growth, in body weight training this is achieved through a progression of exercise intensity. In lifting weights you simply add more weight to the bar, whereas in body weight training you can increase the intensity or overload by slowing down the time it takes to perform each repetition (i.e. from 2 seconds to 4 seconds), otherwise performing a more challenging exercise for the same muscle group by pro-gressing through the 5 Phases outlined. As one exercise becomes easy, you move up to a harder exercise of the same muscle group, so you fall within this 8–12 repetition range or add a weight such as a medicine ball.

Overload in bodyweight abdominal training can also come from rotating exercises, reducing the rest periods between sets as well as going from a stable surface (ie. ground) to an unstable surface (ie. fitness ball) to perform the same exercise. Time on task can also be used as a replacement of repetitions, namely isometric holds or exercises that aim to imitate muscle endurance required for a sports performance (ie. 50 seconds of abdominal crunches to imitate a 400 m run).

As not one routine fits all, having various options available provides the variety required to achieve your goal. Ultimately it becomes a game of trial and error, as some participants will easily surpass the set amount of reps, where others fail. So, aim for the 8–15 repetition range. If you do it easy, change the exercise or simply slow the exercise down so you spend more time under tension. For example, if you can do 12 abdominal crunches easy in 12 seconds, slow it down to perform up to 12 reps in 24 or 36 seconds (2 or 3 seconds each rep) maintaining good form and you will be challenged. In other cases, it will be time on task alone that will increase the exercise intensity.

Ultimately, the variations supplied above will help establish the repetitions and sets to suit your needs for overloading a muscle group for optimal abdominal strength gains. Vary exercises regularly and specific target abdominal muscle regions to maintain this challenge. And remember, always focus on improving the link between weaker and more dominant muscle groups throughout the body for better movement synergy and muscle balance.

Recovery or Rest Periods

Allowing 30–180 seconds recovery is recommended between most exercises, if working the same muscle group or the same exercise is being repeated. In some cases, no rest is required as the exercise targets one muscle region whilst the other has a rest and visa versa. In general, recovery is based on three key elements:

1. Purpose of your training – low, medium or high intensity (endurance, strength or power based)
2. One's current fitness or strength level
3. The type of exercise being performed

Remember, the longer the recovery period the fresher you will be – choose accordingly to suit your needs.

Developing Abdominal Exercise Routines

The following abdominal exercise routines 1–5 are broken down into specific regions that can be trained on different days. *The trunk muscles themselves can be trained everyday if you rotate the routines and are not performing the same exercises in the same movement plane.* If a variety of exercises working all muscle groups are performed on the same day, such as those found in the mixed, advanced, postnatal and sports routines 6–13 a rest day will be required the following day.

1. **Static Exercise Routine**

2. **Upper Abdominal Routine**

3. **Abdominal Obliques Routine**

4. **Lower Abdominal Routine**

5. **Lower Back Routine**

6. **Mixed Routine**

7. **Advanced Routine**

8. **Postnatal Abdominal Routine**

9. **Sports-specific: Balance Sports**

10. **Sports-specific: Ball Sports**

11. **Sports-specific: Golf, Racquet and Bat Sports**

12. **Sports-specific: Running Sports**

13. **Sports-specific: Swimming**

On the following pages fill in the number of sets, repetitions (Reps or time) and rest, based on the advice of a fitness professional or physiotherapist. In general, 3 sets of 8-15 reps with 30-60 seconds rest provides an exercise baseline as well as 1–5 exercises per muscle group or phase depending on your current strength and coordination levels. Abdominal holds may be held whilst maintaining a good

abdominal brace, body position and deep breathing pattern. The idea of an abdominal brace is to avoid any stress being directed to other parts of the body (ie. lower back). This should be avoided at all costs and the exercise stopped whether after 1 second or 1 minute.

Awesome Abs Exercise Guidelines

To ensure safe progress with abdominal training adhere to the following guidelines:

- Gain approval to exercise from your doctor.
- See a physical therapist to assess your posture and joint mechanics and approve appropriate exercises for you.
- Have a physical therapist or certified fitness professional demonstrate each exercise and correct any faults you may have whilst performing them yourself.
- **Recommendation:** All exercises must be performed under the guidance and supervision of a certified fitness professional or physiotherapist.
- Perform exercises in a clear open space free of any obstacles.
- Use an exercise mat where appropriate.
- To help support the lower back region use a LumbAtube™ or half-rolled towel where appropriate.
- Emphasize quality of movement over quantity.
- Get to know your abdominal muscles to understand their function.
- Warm up the body prior to exercising followed by pre-activity stretching.
- Learn neutral spine position for maintaining correct body posture.
- Apply abdominal bracing with each exercise to help support the lower back.

- Maintain a deep breathing pattern with each exercise – never hold your breath.

- Ensure the head and neck maintain a neutral position in line with the lower back at all times.

- Start with Phase 1 and master these drills before progressing to Phase 2 and so forth.

- Avoid any stress or pain on the lower back region. Always stop the exercise instantly if these occur.

- It is important to rotate all abdominal exercises regularly to ensure a challenge is placed on the abdominal region.

- Be sure to include lower back exercise and stretching with each session.

- If at any stage during exercising the abdominal region you feel tension, numbness, dizziness or pain, stop the exercise immediately and seek medical advice.

1. Static Exercise Routine

This routine focuses on improving abdominal bracing, neutral spine position and body awareness. Whilst the exercise demand is low, performing these exercises regularly is crucial in learning muscle motor control and deep breathing.

Exercise	Target Area
1. 4-Point Kneeling Sets: ____ Seconds held:____ Rest: ____	
2. Heel Slide Sets: ____ Reps:____ Rest: ____ **Note:** *Repeat opposite side*	
3. The Hundred Drill Sets: ____ Seconds held:____ Rest: ____	
4. Collins Lateral Hold Sets: ____ Seconds held:____ Rest: ____ **Note:** *Repeat opposite side*	
5. Plank – Elbow Hold Sets: ____ Seconds held:____ Rest: ____	

2. Upper Abdominal Routine

This routine focuses primarily on the rectus abdominis (upper fibers).

Exercise	Target Area
1. Abdominal Slide Sets: ____ Reps:____ Rest: ____	
2. Raised Crunch Sets: ____ Reps:____ Rest: ____	
3. Fitness Ball Crunch Levels 1, 2 or 3 Sets: ____ Reps:____ Rest: ____	
4. Alternate Leg and Arm Raise Sets: ____ Reps:____ Rest: ____	

Recommendation: All exercises must be performed under the guidance and supervision of a certified fitness professional or physiotherapist.

3. Abdominal Obliques Routine

This routine focuses primarily on the internal and external obliques.

Exercise	Target Area
1. Chest Crossovers Sets: _____ Reps:_____ Rest: _____	
2. Lateral Side Raises Sets: _____ Reps:_____ Rest: _____ **Note:** *Repeat opposite side*	
3. Criss-Cross Sets: _____ Reps:_____ Rest: _____	
4. Single Arm Toe Reach Sets: _____ Reps:_____ Rest: _____ **Note:** *Repeat opposite side*	

Recommendation: All exercises must be performed under the guidance and supervision of a certified fitness professional or physiotherapist.

4. Lower Abdominal Routine

This routine focuses primarily on the rectus abdominis (lower fibers) as well as pelvic and hip positioning.

Exercise	Target Area
1. Scissors Sets: _____ Reps:_____ Rest: _____	
2. Body Dish Sets: _____ Reps:_____ Rest: _____	
3. Lower Abdominal Lifts Sets: _____ Reps:_____ Rest: _____	
4. Captains Chair – Knee Raises Sets: _____ Reps:_____ Rest: _____	

Recommendation: All exercises must be performed under the guidance and supervision of a certified fitness professional or physiotherapist.

5. Lower Back Routine

This routine focuses primarily on the lower back and gluteal regions.

Exercise	Target Area
1. Hip Raise Sets: _____ Reps:_____ Rest: _____	
2. Controlled Back Raise Sets: _____ Reps:_____ Rest: _____	
3. Fitness Ball Trunk Extension Sets: _____ Reps:_____ Rest: _____	
4. Fitness Ball – Arm and Leg Raise Sets: _____ Reps:_____ Rest: _____	

Recommendation: All exercises must be performed under the guidance and supervision of a certified fitness professional or physiotherapist.

THE BODY COACH

6. Mixed Abdominal Routine

This mixed routine combines all muscles of the abdominal region.

Exercise	Target Area

1. Abdominal Slide

Sets: ____
Reps:____
Rest: ____

2. Chest Crossovers

Sets: ____
Reps:____
Rest: ____

3. Lateral Side Raises

Sets: ____
Reps:____
Rest: ____

Note: *Repeat opposite side*

4. Fitness Ball Crunch

Levels 1, 2 or 3

Sets: ____
Reps:____
Rest: ____

Exercise	Target Area

5. Body Dish

Sets: _____
Reps: _____
Rest: _____

6. Lower Abdominal Lifts

Sets: _____
Reps: _____
Rest: _____

7. Fitness Ball Trunk Extension

Sets: _____
Reps: _____
Rest: _____

8. Fitness Ball –
Arm and Leg Raise

Sets: _____
Reps: _____
Rest: _____

Recommendation: All exercises must be performed under the guidance and supervision of a certified fitness professional or physiotherapist.

7. Advanced Abdominal Routine

This advanced routine requires a high level of focus, commitment and quality in each exercise to ensure proper form is maintained.

Exercise	Target Area

1. Collins Lateral Hold

Sets: _____
Seconds held:_____
Rest: _____

Note: *Repeat opposite side*

2. The Hundred Drill

Sets: _____
Seconds held:_____
Rest: _____

3. Lateral Side Raises

Sets: _____
Reps:_____
Rest: _____

Note: *Repeat opposite side*

4. Fitness Ball Crunch

Levels 1, 2 or 3

Sets: _____
Reps:_____
Rest: _____

Exercise	Target Area

5. Hanging Knee Raises

Sets: _____
Reps: _____
Rest: _____

6. Weighted toe Touches

Sets: _____
Reps: _____
Rest: _____

7. Power Jumps

Sets: _____
Reps: _____
Rest: _____

8. Dumbbell Front Raise

Sets: _____
Reps: _____
Rest: _____

Recommendation: All exercises must be performed under the guidance and supervision of a certified fitness professional or physiotherapist.

THE BODY COACH

8. Postnatal Abdominal Routine

This routine assists moms in restrengthening their abdominal muscles starting eight weeks after childbirth. Before attempting, gain clearance from your doctor to see whether these exercises are suitable for you.

Exercise	Target Area
1. 4-Point Kneeling Sets: ____ Seconds held:____ Rest: ____	
2. Heel Slide Sets: ____ Reps:____ Rest: ____ **Note:** *Repeat opposite side*	
3. Abdominal Slide Sets: ____ Reps:____ Rest: ____	
4. Chest Crossovers Sets: ____ Reps:____ Rest: ____	

9. Sports-specific: Balance Sports

This routine is focused on sports such as cycling, ice-skating, skateboarding, snowboarding, snow-skiing, surfing, wake-boarding, waterskiing.

Exercise	Target Area
1. Plank – Elbow Hold Sets: ____ Seconds held:____ Rest: ____	
2. Medicine Ball Coordination Crunch Sets: ____ Reps:____ Rest: ____	
3. Collins Lateral Hold Sets: ____ Seconds held:____ Rest: ____ **Note:** *Repeat opposite side*	
4. Reverse Curls Sets: ____ Reps:____ Rest: ____	
5. Elbow to Knee (weighted) Sets: ____ Seconds held:____ Rest: ____ **Note:** *Repeat opposite side*	

10. Sports-specific: Ball Sports

This routine is focused on sports such as basketball, handball, netball, NFL, rugby, soccer, volleyball and waterpolo.

Exercise	Target Area

1. Weighted Arm Extensions

Sets: _____
Reps:_____
Rest: _____

2. Weighted Toe Touches

Sets: _____
Reps:_____
Rest: _____

3. Lateral Side Raises

Sets: _____
Reps:_____
Rest: _____

Note: *Repeat opposite side*

4. Plank – Elbow Hold

Sets: _____
Seconds held:_____
Rest: _____

5. Lower Abdominal Lifts

Sets: _____
Reps:_____
Rest: _____

11. Sports-specific: Golf, Racquet & Bat Sports

This routine is focused on sports such as badminton, baseball, cricket, golf, hockey, lacrosse, softball, squash and tennis.

Exercise	Target Area
1. Collins Lateral Hold Sets: _____ Seconds held:_____ Rest: _____ **Note:** *Repeat opposite side*	
2. Abdominal Slide Sets: _____ Reps:_____ Rest: _____	
3. Criss-Cross Sets: _____ Reps:_____ Rest: _____	
4. Reverse Curls Sets: _____ Reps:_____ Rest: _____	
5. Medicine Ball Isometric Twists Sets: _____ Reps:_____ Rest: _____	

12. Sports-specific: Running Sports

This sports specific routine is focused on running sports such as athletics, NFL, rugby, soccer and alike.

Exercise	Target Area
1. Lower Abdominal Lifts Sets: ____ Reps:____ Rest: ____	
2. Chest Crossovers Sets: ____ Reps:____ Rest: ____	
3. The Hundred Drill Sets: ____ Seconds held:____ Rest: ____	
4. Collins Plank Pattern Sets: ____ Reps:____ Rest: ____	
5. Hanging Knee/Leg Raises Sets: ____ Reps:____ Rest: ____	

13. Sports-specific: Swimming

This sports specific routine is focused on swimming with the primary focus on lower abdominals and obliques for good starts, strong turns and maintaining good body position in the water over extended periods.

Exercise	Target Area

1. Captains Chair – Knee Raises

Sets: _____
Reps: _____
Rest: _____

2. Collins Lateral Hold

Sets: _____
Seconds held: _____
Rest: _____

Note: *Repeat opposite side*

3. Fitness Ball Crunch
Levels 1, 2 or 3

Sets: _____
Reps: _____
Rest: _____

4. Lateral Side Raises

Sets: _____
Reps: _____
Rest: _____

Note: *Repeat opposite side*

5. Lower Abdominal Lifts

Sets: _____
Reps: _____
Rest: _____

Design Your Own Abdominal Training Routine

After testing your core-body strength and finding your strength and weaknesses return to the respective exercises for each abdominal muscle group (or phase) to help design a program that develops a strong abdominal core region suitable to your needs.

The reps, sets, recovery and exercises need to be adjusted regularly to ensure a challenge is placed on the targeted muscle groups. Use the following chart to assist in designing your own core-strength training routine. Record your training goal in the top section of the table for motivation and direction in your training.

Abdominal Routine

My training goal is:				
Exercise	Page No.	Reps	Sets	Recovery
1				
2				
3				
4				
5				
6				
7				
8				

www.thebodycoach.com

International Managing Agent

Saxton Speakers Bureau (Australia)

- Website: www.saxton.com.au
- Email: speakers@saxton.com.au
- Phone: (03) 9811 3500
  International: +61 3 9811 3500

www.thebodycoach.com

Study in Australia

- International Fitness College for overseas students to study sport, fitness and personal training qualifications in Sydney Australia
- 3 month to 2 year student visa courses

www.sportandfitness.com.au

AUSTRALIAN ACADEMY OF SPORT AND FITNESS

Abdominal Index

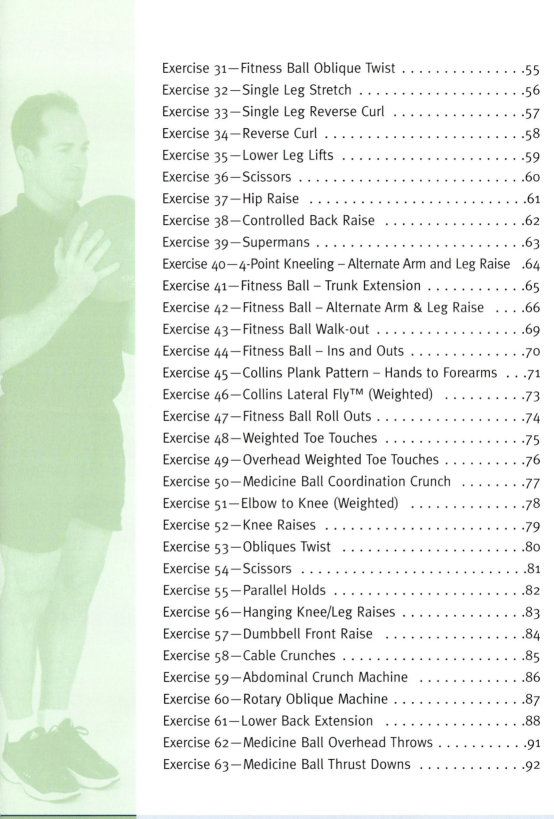

Abdominal Exercise Routines

Photo & Illustration Credits

Cover Design: Jens Vogelsang
Photos: Paul Collins

The Body Coach

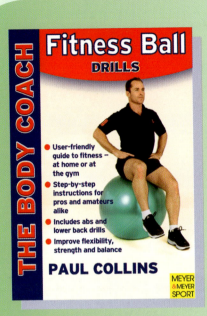

Paul Collins
Fitness Ball Drills

Fitness Ball Drills is a user-friendly exercise guide for achieving a stronger, leaner and more flexible body. The Fitness Ball is one of the most utilized pieces of gym and fitness equipment used throughout the world to tone, stretch and strengthen the whole body. Body Coach Paul Collins provides step-by-step coaching for improving posture, balance, coordination, strength and flexibility with more than 50 exercises that can easily be carried out at home or in the gym. Fitness Ball Drills is the perfect book for those who seek to improve their total body fitness.

144 pages, full-color print
182 color photos
Paperback, 6¹/₂" x 9¹/₄"
ISBN: 978-1-84126-221-5
$ 14.95 US/$ 20.95 CDN
£ 9.95 UK/€ 14.95

www.m-m-sports.com

pursue

a 9-week small group collision

Knowing the Messiah

Standard
PUBLISHING

Cincinnati, Ohio

CD-ROM with printable student pages enclosed

pursue

Published by Standard Publishing, Cincinnati, Ohio
www.standardpub.com

Copyright © 2010 by CHRIST IN YOUTH

Also available:
Redefining the Win for Jr. High Small Groups, ISBN 978-0-7847-2320-3, copyright © 2010 by CHRIST IN YOUTH
Connect, ISBN 978-0-7847-2405-7, copyright © 2010 by CHRIST IN YOUTH
Speak, ISBN 978-0-7847-2406-4, copyright © 2010 by CHRIST IN YOUTH

Printed in: United States of America
Project editor: Kelly Carr
Cover and interior design: Thinkpen Design, Inc., www.thinkpendesign.com

ISBN 978-0-7847-2407-1

15 14 13 12 11 10   1 2 3 4 5 6 7 8 9